KNOWLEDGE ENCYCLOPEDIA
EARTH
DISCOVERIES
INVENTIONS & DISCOVERIES

(An imprint of Prakash Books Pvt. Ltd.)

Wonder House Books
Corporate & Editorial Office
113-A, 1st Floor, Ansari Road,
Daryaganj, New Delhi-110002
Tel +91 11 2324 7062-65

Printed in 2020 in India

ISBN : 9789390391110

Table of Contents

MAPPING EARTH

Human beings began large-scale explorations of Earth some 4,000 years ago.
The European Age of Discovery, however, began during the 15th century. During
this time, Europeans strove to discover and colonise lands that could make them
rich. Their explorations led to an increase in their knowledge of the New World,
the polar regions and the southern hemisphere. They discovered new ocean routes
and islands. Their many adventures led to scientific discoveries that revolutionised
the world. Their commercial motives also led to empire building, war, prejudice
and slavery. In the 20th century, satellite images filled in details of the last unknown
parts of Earth.

▼ *A map of the world from 1733 shows nothing but water around the
poles. The Arctic and Antarctic expeditions were dangerous adventures
undertaken by only the hardiest, most determined explorers*

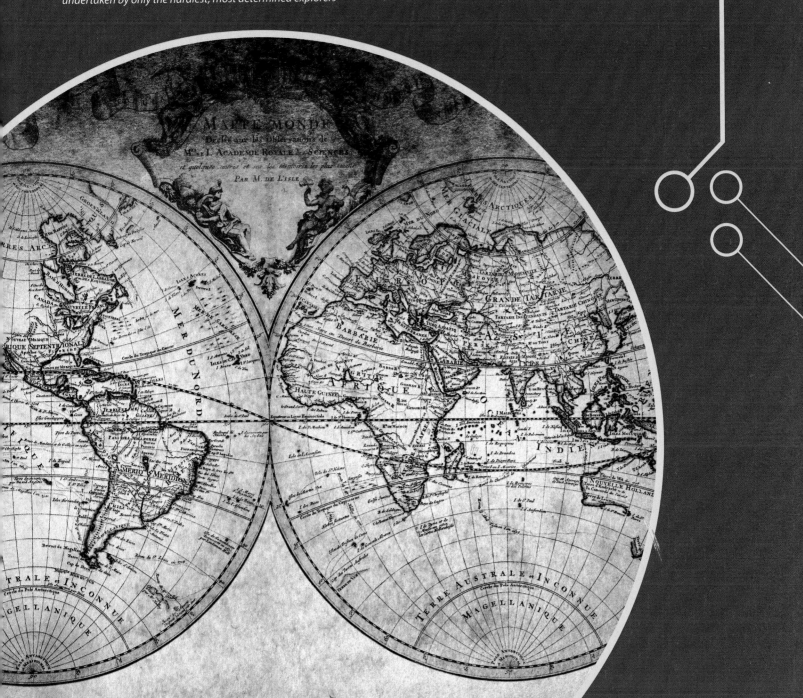

The Adventures of Marco Polo

Italian merchant Marco Polo (1254–1324 CE) introduced the fabled worlds of China and Asia to medieval Europe. Marco belonged to a family of jewel merchants who traded with Eastern nations. In 1271, he journeyed with his father and uncle (Niccolo and Maffeo Polo) to the powerful Mongol kingdom. Marco Polo was just 17 years old. Over the next 24 years, he would acquire incredible knowledge of Asia and Europe through his fantastic travels.

▲ An 1867 mosaic of Marco Polo at the Palazzo Grimaldi Doria-Tursi (the Municipal Palace of Genoa)

🔍 The Legendary Silk Road

Carrying letters from the Pope to the Mongol Emperor Kublai Khan, Marco and his relatives journeyed through the wealthy city of Acre into south-eastern Turkey and northern Iran. They crossed hostile bandit-infested deserts and rested at Hormuz, a city on the Persian **Gulf**. The Polos then continued into Asia using the Silk Road.

The legendary Silk Road was a string of valuable trade routes across China, India and the Mediterranean. Large convoys of wealth-laden caravans were a common sight here. They were often accompanied by armed cohorts to guard the riches. The Polos visited fabulous places like Khorasan, Badakhshan, Pamir, Kota and even the Gobi Desert. Finally, in 1275, they reached Chengdu, where they met Kublai Khan at his summer palace.

▼ Marco Polo's route from Venice (Italy) to Mongol China (then known as Cathay to the West)

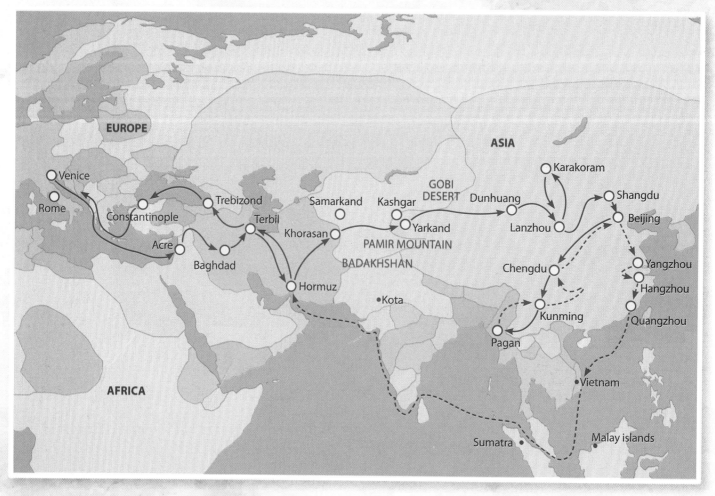

⭐ Incredible Individuals

Young Marco was amazed by the opulence of Mongol China. Nothing in Europe quite compared to it. The Khan's capital city, **Kinsay**, was large, clean and organised. It had wide roads and extraordinary infrastructure—like the Grand Canal, which is, even today, the largest man-made waterway. The food, the clothes, the people and the animals were all new and fascinating to Marco. In his book, he wrote of rhinoceroses and crocodiles, which he thought were unicorns and giant, toothed serpents (with "eyes bigger than a four penny loaf")!

▶ *An engraving of Marco Polo*

🔍 The Khan's Favourite

Marco was about 20 years old when he reached China. He would live there for another 17 years. He became a favourite of Kublai Khan, who loved listening to his stories of far-off lands. In fact, the emperor sent Marco to explore different parts of his own empire. Eventually, Marco held official posts at court. He even claimed to be the governor of Yangzhou for about three years.

🔍 Journey Home

Around 1290–1292 CE, Kublai Khan sent a princess-bride to Argun Khan of Persia. She was accompanied by 600 courtiers and 14 ships. Reluctantly, he also allowed the Polos to leave in her train. They visited Vietnam, the Malay islands and Sumatra, before reaching Persia. From there, the Polos travelled on to Trebizond (where they were badly robbed) and Constantinople. They reached home in Venice, in 1295.

▲ *Soon after his death in 1294, Kublai Khan was painted (as a younger man) by the Nepalese artist and astronomer Anige. This silk painting can be seen at the National Palace Museum in Taiwan*

🔍 Il Milione

In 1298, Marco Polo became a prisoner of war. That year, he narrated his stories to a fellow prisoner, Rustichello. The tales were published and became hugely popular. For the first time in centuries, Europeans learned what the East was really like. The amazing book, *Il Milione* is more commonly known as *The Travels of Marco Polo* in English.

👤 In Real Life

The maps that Marco Polo brought back from his journey influenced the development of **cartography** and are still used as a guide to undiscovered archaeological sites.

▲ *The 15th century monk Fra Mauro's map of the world—the most accurate map of that time—owed a great deal to a nautical map and a world map that Polo brought back from his travels*

▲ *Marco Polo passed away at the age of 70 in Venice. He lies buried at the Campo San Lorenzo*

China's Exploration of the 'West'

One of China's greatest admirals and diplomats, Zheng He (1371–1433) commanded seven epic sea voyages. He extended China's influence over the Indian ocean and parts of Africa and the Middle East.

🔍 Emperor Yongle's Mission

By 1368 CE, the Mongol rulers of China had been overthrown. A new Ming dynasty held the throne. Zheng He was only 10 years old when his Mongol home was lost to war. Forced to join the Ming army, he grew into a strong and diplomatic warrior. By 1390 CE, he had powerful friends in the imperial court. When the emperor wanted to conquer the 'Western Oceans', he chose Zheng He to lead the navy.

▲ *Statue of the Yongle Emperor in Ling En Hall of Changling tomb, in Ming Dynasty Tombs, Beijing*

🔍 The Indian Ocean

The first voyage, over 1405–1407, began with 62 ships and 27,800 men. Zheng He visited Champa (southern Vietnam), Siam (Thailand), Malacca and Java. He then travelled to the wealthy port of Calicut in India and to Ceylon (Sri Lanka). In 1408–1409, Zheng He returned to India and Ceylon. However, he ended up in a battle with Ceylon's King Alagonakkara. Zheng He defeated the king and took him back as a prisoner to China.

◄ *A statue of Zheng He at the Quanzhou Maritime Museum*

▶ *A 17th-century Chinese woodblock print of Zheng He's ships*

⚙ Incredible Individuals

Zheng He was born as Ma Sanbao to a Chinese Muslim family. His devout father made the Hajj **pilgrimage** to Mecca. Their name Ma is a Chinese word that comes from 'Muhammad'. Later in life, Zheng He became more interested in Buddhism.

▶ *Sculpture of a young Zheng He with his father Ma Hajji*

🔍 Arabia and Africa

In October 1409, Zheng He took to the seas again. He sailed all the way to Hormuz on the Persian Gulf. On his return in 1411, he touched the northern tip of Sumatra. During his fourth **expedition**, in 1413, he went farther down the Arabian coast to Dhofar (Oman) and Aden (Yemen). The mission took him to Mecca, Egypt and to modern-day Somalia and Kenya. By 1415, Zheng He was back before the Chinese emperor. He brought **envoys** or **ambassadors** from more than 30 states to pay respect to the emperor.

🔍 The Final Forays

The fifth voyage, over 1417–1419, was to the Persian Gulf and East Africa. In 1421, the sixth voyage was launched to send foreign ambassadors home. Around this time, a new emperor came to power. He put a stop to these missions. However, Zheng He made one final voyage in the winter of 1431 to southeast Asia, India, the Persian Gulf, the Red Sea and Eastern Africa. On the return trip, he passed away in Calicut in the spring of 1433.

◀ *Indonesia issued special stamps to commemorate the 600th anniversary of Admiral Zheng He's voyage*

💡 Isn't It Amazing!

Zheng He's fleets carried priceless **lacquerware**, porcelains and silks made by Ming craftsmen. These were traded at different ports for gems, spices, ivory, aromatics, herbs and other valuable items. Zheng He even brought back a giraffe to China!

▲ *The well-travelled giraffe of the Sultan of Bengal was originally brought from the Somali Ajuran Empire. It was eventually taken to China in the 13th year of the Yongle Emperor*

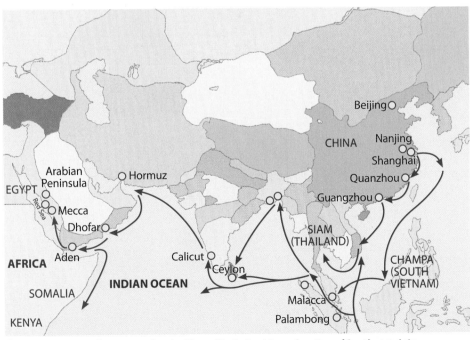

▲ *The map shows the routes taken by Zheng He during his exploration of Southeast Asia, India, Middle East and Africa*

▲ *Zheng He's tomb in Nanjing, China*

A Passage to India

The infamous Portuguese navigator Vasco da Gama (1460–1524) opened up a new sea route from Europe to India. This took him around the Cape of Good Hope, which is located in the south of the continent of Africa. Its name comes from a belief of ancient travellers that India could be reached by sea from Europe. Vasco da Gama sailed for King Manuel I of Portugal, who wanted to control the riches of India.

▲ *King Manuel I directs a kneeling Vasco da Gama to sail to India*

🔍 The First Voyage: 1497–1499

Da Gama left Lisbon with four ships on 8 July, 1497. After battling storms and scurvy, they sailed into Calicut on 20 May, 1498. Calicut was then a wealthy port-city on India's western coast. Its powerful ruler, the Zamorin, courteously received the Portuguese sailors. But in return, da Gama offered cheap gifts. He even tried selling poor-quality items to the savvy city merchants. Naturally, people refused his offers and looked down upon him. A sulking da Gama left by the end of August, vowing revenge.

💡 Isn't It Amazing!

On this first voyage, da Gama was away for over two years. He spent 300 days at sea and travelled about 39,000 kilometres.

▲ *An 1850 engraving shows da Gama greeting the Zamorin, the king of Calicut*

👤✓ In Real Life

Da Gama's ships carried stone pillars meant to mark 'discovered' territories, even though the regions were already inhabited by **indigenous** populations.

▲ *Arriving from Lisbon, Portugal to Kochi (formerly Cochin), India*

🔍 The Second Voyage: 1502–1503 CE

Da Gama returned to India with an armed fleet, intent on wreaking havoc. He began by stealing the cargo of an Arab ship and setting its 200–400 passengers (men, women and children) on fire! With the help of Cannore (Kannur) and Cochin (Kochi)—enemies of Calicut—he forced the Zamorin to agree to his terms. Da Gama sailed back to Portugal with shiploads of ill-gotten gains.

🔍 The Last Voyage: 1524 CE

In 1524, da Gama returned as the Portuguese Viceroy of India. However, he fell ill and died in Kochi. In 1538, his body was sent back to Portugal.

◀ *Vasco da Gama's pillar in Kenya, used to commemorate his 'discovery' of the land*

The New World

The 15th-century Italian explorer Christopher Columbus is often credited with discovering the Americas. However, many others were there before him—notably the Vikings and the Native Americans. Columbus's achievement was bringing the Americas into wider public consciousness. His ambition kicked off global territorial battles. In the same century, a Spanish **conquistador** named Vasco Nunez de Balboa established the first stable settlement in the New World and 'discovered' its eastern (Pacific Ocean) shores.

▲ *In the 16th century, Italian explorer Amerigo Vespucci first realised that South America was a proper continent and not an extension of Asia. He thus called it the New World. He also discovered present-day Brazil*

A Permanent Settlement

In 1510, Balboa, a failing planter and pig farmer in Haiti, escaped his creditors by hiding in a ship's barrel (along with his dog Leoncico)! The ship brought him to the Spanish settlement of Uraba (in modern Colombia). The settlement eventually moved to the Isthmus of Panama. There, they defeated 500 Native Americans led by chief Cemaco and established Santa Maria la Antigua del Darien, the first permanent settlement of Europeans on the American mainland.

◄ *Columbus lands on the West Indies and claims the territory for imperial Spain, while ignoring the fact that the land was already home to many indigenous people*

Panama and the Pacific

In 1515, Balboa sailed from Santa Maria to Acla, the narrowest part of the **Isthmus** of Panama. He was hunting for a rumoured gold-rich province. Balboa brought along 190 Spaniards and hundreds of porters. They travelled southwards through deep forests, crossing rivers and swamps and ascending a mountain range. On 25 September, 1513 (though part of the travel record also states 27 September as the date), standing "silent, upon a peak in Darien", Balboa found himself looking at the Pacific Ocean.

The South Sea

A group led by Alonso Martin became the first to actually reach the Pacific shore. Balboa himself arrived on 29 September. He walked into the sea with a holy flag and a sword. Taking possession of the new sea for the King of Castille, he named it the Mar del Sur (South Sea).

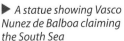

▲ *The modern Port of Balboa on the Panama Canal, built over the 19th and 20th centuries*

▶ *A statue showing Vasco Nunez de Balboa claiming the South Sea*

Shortcuts and Roundtrips

Sailing for the king of Spain, Ferdinand Magellan (1480–1521) was the first European to discover the sea route that goes below South America. The passage is named after him as the **Strait** of Magellan. It became Europe's shortcut to the Pacific Ocean. Magellan's ship—under the leadership of Juan Sebastian del Cano—was also the first to fully circumnavigate Earth.

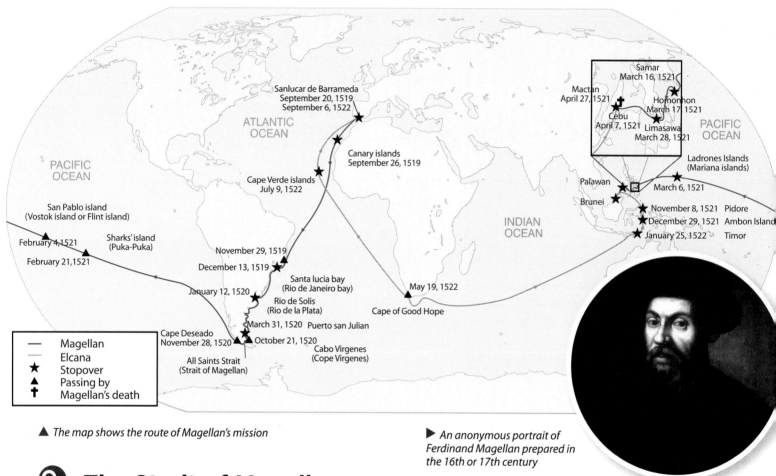

▲ *The map shows the route of Magellan's mission*

▶ *An anonymous portrait of Ferdinand Magellan prepared in the 16th or 17th century*

🔍 The Strait of Magellan

Like many explorers of his time, Magellan believed that one could sail to the Pacific Ocean through a shortcut across South America. On 20 September, 1519, he left Spain with five ships: the *Trinidad*, *San Antonio*, *Concepcion*, *Santiago* and *Victoria*.

Over the next year, they explored the waterways of Argentina, searching for a strait that cut across to the Pacific. On 21 October, 1520, Magellan rounded the Cape of the Virgins. He entered the strait that would later bear his name. When he received news that the Pacific Ocean had been sighted, the iron-willed admiral broke down and cried with joy.

💡 Isn't It Amazing!

In 1966–1967, British adventurer Francis Charles Chichester completed the first solo circumnavigation of Earth. He was sailing the yacht, *Gipsy Moth IV*.

👤 In Real Life

About seven months into the journey, three of Magellan's ship captains mutinied. Magellan executed the captain of the *Victoria*. He then cut loose the *Concepcion's* anchor. As the ship drifted towards Magellan's own *Trinidad*, Captain Gaspar Quesada panicked and surrendered. The last captain, Juan de Cartagena of the *San Antonio*, also gave up.

Magellan **marooned** and executed some of the mutineers, but most were forgiven.

The Pacific Crossing

It was a parched, ill and starving fleet that journeyed across the Pacific Ocean. The crews were surviving on rat-bitten biscuits and hard leather, but a determined Magellan kept them on course. After 99 days, they finally reached Guam and obtained fresh food. Magellan then steered towards the Philippines, where, in 1521, the catholic Raja Hamabon of Cebu became the first Pacific Island ruler to accept an alliance with Spain. Just weeks later, Magellan found himself in a battle on Mactan island. He was wounded by a bamboo spear, surrounded and killed.

Incredible Individuals

Magellan was equal in skill to Vasco da Gama as a sailor, but many scholars tracking the history of Portugal overlook him as he sailed for the king of Spain. Historians from Spain overlook him as well, choosing to give credit to the discoveries of another navigator named Cano. However, Magellan's discoveries would not have been made without the patronage of the Spanish king.

◀ Magellan's battle and death in the Philippines

▼ Shrine to Magellan at Mactan

Proving Earth is Round

After Magellan's death, only two of his ships remained—the *Trinidad* and the *Victoria*. The *Trinidad* was no longer seaworthy. Cano, originally a member of the *Concepcion*, took charge of the *Victoria* and reached Spain on 8 September, 1522. He thus conclusively showed that Earth was indeed a globe. Emperor Charles added on Cano's coat of arms the inscription '*Primus circumdedisti me*', which translated to 'You were the first to encircle me'.

▲ The *Victoria* was the only one of Magellan's five ships to circumnavigate the globe

Exploring North America

English explorer Henry Hudson (1565–1611) is famous for his discoveries of the region around present-day New York. Hudson's journeys began as a search for an ice-free shortcut to Japan and China, by way of the North Pole. He set off in 1607 with his son John and ten others. On this voyage, he explored the polar ice front as far east as the Svalbard archipelago. He set out again on 22 April, 1608, exploring the area between Svalbard and Novaya Zemlya islands, east of the Barents Sea. Unfortunately, he was forced to return after finding his path blocked by ice.

▲ *Aerial view of New York City and the Hudson River*

🔍 The Hudson River

In 1609, Hudson embarked on his third voyage on the ship *Half Moon*. While navigating the Atlantic shores, he encountered a vast river that had already been discovered in 1524 by Florentine navigator Giovanni da Verrazzano. However, this would eventually be called the Hudson River. By September, Hudson had passed Cape Cod, Chesapeake **Bay** and Delaware Bay and reached the river's **estuary** without discovering any route to the Pacific.

▲ *A replica of the Dutch ship Halve Maen (Half Moon)*

▶ *Henry Hudson's statue in Henry Hudson Park*

🔍 Hudson Bay

Hudson's next journey led him to an inlet of water that would later be known as Hudson Strait. Sailing on the *Discovery* on 17 April, 1610, Hudson stopped briefly in Iceland, then passed through the straits to Hudson Bay. Exploring it thoroughly, he landed in James Bay (the southern end of Hudson Bay), still finding no outlet to the Pacific.

Hudson eventually got stranded there for the winter. Quarrels arose among his people. On 22 June, 1611, mutineers set Hudson and his son adrift on a small open boat. Neither of them were seen again. The ringleaders of the **mutiny** were themselves killed by Inuits before they reached home.

▲ *The Last Voyage of Henry Hudson, a painting by John Collier*

◀ *Henry Hudson entering New York bay on 11 September, 1609, with a Native American family watching from the shore*

The Lands Down Under

Dutch navigator Abel Janszoon Tasman (1603–1659) was the first European to discover Tasmania, New Zealand, Tonga and the Fiji Islands. For most of his life, Tasman was based in Batavia (now Jakarta), where he kept a lookout for rebels and smugglers. In 1642, Tasman was commissioned to explore the southern stretches of the Indian Ocean and map its lands.

Tasmania and New Zealand

On 16 August, 1642, Tasman embarked with two ships—the *Heemskerk* and the *Zeehaen*—to Mauritius. Sailing south and east, he discovered new land on 24 November, which he named Van Diemen's Land (Tasmania). On 13 December, Tasman and his crew became the first Europeans to sight New Zealand's South Island. They entered the strait between North and South Islands, exploring Murderers Bay, North Island's coasts, the Cook Strait, Cape Maria Van Diemen and the Three Kings islands. They spent Christmas just east of Stephens and D'Urville islands.

In Real Life

This was the first time the Maori people of New Zealand saw Europeans. Tasman and seven crewmen tried to land on a small boat, but the Maori attacked them, killing three and leaving a fourth to die of wounds. Tasman thus named this area Murderers Bay.

◀ *A drawing by Isaack Gilsemans, Tasman's artist, illustrating the Dutch team surrounded by the Maori people at Murderers Bay (now Golden Bay), New Zealand*

Tonga and Fiji

Sailing northeast, Tasman discovered Tonga on 21 January and the Fiji Islands on 6 February. The ships then turned west and sailed back to Batavia through the New Guinea waters. The whole trip took 10 months and Tasman went around Australia without ever seeing it!

Australia

In 1644, Tasman embarked on a new expedition to search for a southern continent. This time, he steered southeast below New Guinea, through the Torres Strait and into Australia's Gulf of Carpentaria. Coasting along, Tasman was able to map the northern coast of Australia.

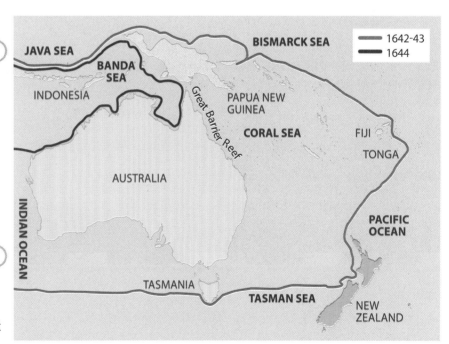

▲ *The map shows the route of Abel Tasman's first and second exploratory voyage around New Zealand and Australia. The first voyage was taken between 1642–43 and the second voyage was taken in 1644*

James Cook

Have you heard of James Cook (1728–1779)? He was a British navy captain famous for his explorations of Antarctica, Australia and New Zealand in the south, and the Bering Strait and North America in the north. More amazingly, he set new benchmarks in seamanship, navigation and map-making. He modernised attitudes regarding indigenous peoples and the care of sailors at sea. Cook peacefully changed the map of the world more than anyone else in history.

▲ Official portrait of James Cook at the National Maritime Museum

The Southern Hemisphere

In 1768, 40-year-old James Cook was made commander of a scientific expedition to the Pacific. Cook's job was to transport scientists of the Royal Society to Tahiti. And from there, to discover the mysterious southern continent, Terra Australis. Cook commanded HMS *Endeavour*, while the scientific mission itself was under the leadership of the wealthy 26-year-old scientist Joseph Banks.

◀ Sir Joseph Banks (in the red coat), Captain James Cook (holding out his hat) with other British scientists and aristocrats

▶ A replica of HMS Endeavour at Cooktown Harbour, Australia

Claiming Australia

Over six months in 1769, Cook thoroughly mapped New Zealand. Crossing west on the Tasman Sea, he arrived on Australia's southeast coast on 19 April, 1770, becoming the first European to see this part of the continent. Cook named the area New South Wales and anchored at Botany Bay.

Exploring the 3200-kilometre area to the north from the coast, he even navigated the hazardous Great Barrier Reef, the Coral Sea and the Torres Strait. On 22 August, 1770, Cook claimed the eastern Australian coast for King George III and Britain.

▶ On 14 February, 1779, James Cook got into a fight with Hawaiians over a stolen boat. In the fracas, Cook was struck on the head and slain on the beach at Kealakekua

Isn't It Amazing!

Joseph Banks's mission was such a scientific success, it inspired other scientists to explore the world. Among them were Charles Darwin, Thomas Henry Huxley and Joseph Dalton Hooker, whose voyages and works popularised the theory of evolution.

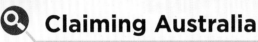

🔍 Measuring Antarctica

Over 1772–1775, Cook sailed out with two ships called the *Resolution* and the *Adventure*. He completed the first west-east circumnavigation near the Antarctic. He discovered New Caledonia in the Pacific, as well as the Atlantic's South Sandwich Islands and South Georgia island. Cook concluded that only the Terra Australis existed in Australia and New Zealand; the rest were frozen lands of Antarctica.

▶ On 11 June, 1770, the Endeavour careened as she struck a coral spur. This part of the Great Barrier Reef has since been called the Endeavour Reef. Cook landed at the mouth of the Endeavour River in Queensland to repair the damages and set off again

▼ *Captain Cook's map of the southern hemisphere with the South Pole at the centre*

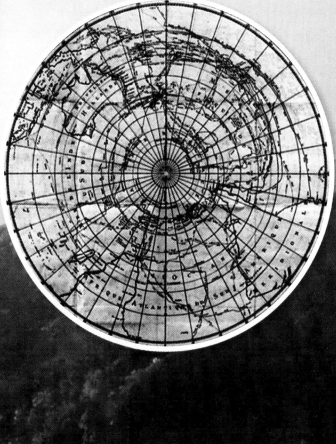

⊙ Incredible Individuals

Ships on long voyages used to have high death tolls owing to a disease called scurvy. This was essentially caused by a lack of Vitamin C, which was unknown in the 18th century. Cook lost none of his men to scurvy and only a few to fever and dysentery. This is because he was strict about cleanliness and ventilation in the sailors' quarters. He insisted that his team follow a diet of cress, sauerkraut and orange extract, all high in Vitamin C. He thus became famous in naval circles for keeping his crew alive and healthy.

The Resolution and Adventure enter Matavai Bay, off the Pacific Ocean

The Lewis and Clark Expedition

In 1803, the USA bought 21,00,000 square kilometres of land from Napoleon in the famous Louisiana Purchase. President Thomas Jefferson sent a mission to explore this new territory via the Missouri River. The expedition was led by his secretary Meriwether Lewis and Lewis's military superior William Clark.

🔍 An Epic Expedition

On 14 May, 1804, they set off with four dozen people, and a dog named Seamen, from St Louis. They sailed along the Missouri River on a 17-metre keelboat and two smaller boats. The mission would eventually cover 13,000 kilometres of pristine lands. At the time, they were populated by vast herds, abundant vegetation and largely peaceful tribes. Over the next 2 years, 4 months and 10 days, the **corps** would experience many adventures before returning to St Louis on 23 September, 1806.

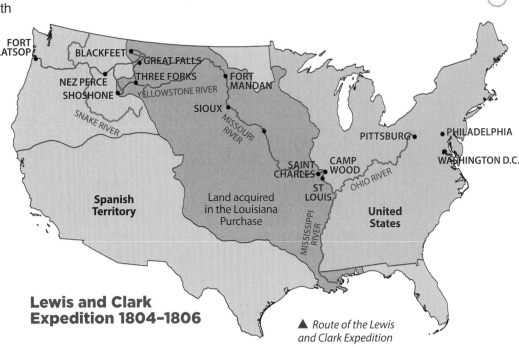

Lewis and Clark Expedition 1804–1806

▲ Route of the Lewis and Clark Expedition

▲ The Great Falls of Missouri River

▲ After leaving the Great Falls, the expedition came across extraordinary cliffs and named them Gates of the Rocky Mountains

🔍 Amazing Discoveries

They documented around 178 new plants, including *prairie sagebrush, Douglas fir* and *ponderosa pine*. Plants were often named after the men, for instance, *Lewisia rediviva* (bitterroot), *Philadelphus lewisii* (mock orange) and *Clarkia pucella* (ragged robin). The grizzly bear, prairie dog, pronghorn antelope and about 122 other animals were also found. The crew named new places after themselves, their loved ones and even after their dogs (Seaman's Creek).

Diplomatic Successes

Lewis and Clark impressed the Native Americans, who were largely welcoming. In return for food, information, guides and shelter, the expedition put on military parades, presented gifts and offered greater trade and peace. There was even a 'magic show' with magnets, compasses and an air gun. The expedition would leave cordially after issuing diplomatic invitations to Washington DC.

Independence Day

In June 1805, Lewis reached a fork in the river. Taking the main south fork, he arrived at the Great Falls. The group had to carry their goods 29 kilometres around the falls over broken, cacti-infested ground and past a number of grizzly bears. They completed the crossing on 4 July, in time to celebrate Independence Day by drinking and dancing the night away.

▲ *In August 1805, Sacagawea's brother, the Shoshone tribe's Chief Cameahwait, helped the expedition purchase horses and find a path through the Rocky Mountains*

◀ *Passing through the Gates, they arrived at the beautiful Three Forks, where the Missouri meets the Jefferson (seen here), Gallantin and Madison rivers*

Isn't It Amazing!

On 8 January, 1806, Clark and Sacagawea found a whale skeleton on a beach. They bought **blubber** and oil from the Native Americans who were processing the whale.

Sacagawea, The Explorer

A member of the Shoshone tribe, Sacagawea joined the expedition as the wife of its member Toussaint Charbonneau. She was then 15 years old and pregnant. Sacagawea proved to be invaluable as an interpreter, negotiator and a path-finder. She even showed the group how to find and cook local foods. Her calm and quick thinking saved the mission many times. When she eventually passed away, Clark adopted her two children Jean Baptiste and Lizette. Since 2000, the US treasury has minted a dollar coin named the Sacagawea Dollar in her honour.

◀ *Sacagawea with her son Jean Baptiste, who was born during the expedition*

▲ *Over July and August 1806, the crew explored Yellow River and the area around it. In another month, they would be home*

▲ *In July, Clark named a majestic rock outcrop Pompey's Tower (now, Pompey's Pillar) after Sacagawea's son, who was affectionately nicknamed Pomp. Clark also carved his own name and date on the Pillar*

The Evolution Revolution

At the age of 22, Englishman Charles Darwin (1809–1882) set sail on HMS *Beagle*. On the way, he spent many months exploring the islands and coasts around South America. Here, Darwin noticed strong patterns between life on the islands and on the main continent. For instance, he saw daisies and sunflowers on an island that were as large as trees!

Charles Darwin ▶

Darwin's Findings

Darwin realised that plants and animals on the islands must have changed to take advantage of the homes they were provided. Thus, on an island that had no trees, the sunflowers evolved to become its trees. Darwin called this the 'theory of natural selection'. He realised that it made plants and animals successful at conquering new environments. This supported the groundbreaking idea that life was not created by God; instead, it evolved over thousands and thousands of years from interactions with nature.

◀ *A series of skulls show how human beings evolved from our ape-like ancestors*

◀ *The frigate bird lives near tropical oceans. Its wings evolved to take advantage of warm currents of air that rise upwards. The bird can thus soar without flapping its wings for hours and even days at a time*

In Real Life

Genes are proteins in our bodies that decide whether we become a plant, a mouse, a human being, or something else. We inherit our genes from our ancestors. Did you know that 98 per cent of our genes are the same as a chimpanzee's? We share 92 per cent of our genes with mice. About half our genes are the same as a fly's. 18 per cent of our genes are the same as some weeds.

Voyage of the Beagle

On 27 December, 1831, HMS *Beagle* set sail for South America. Her captain Robert Fitzroy was an aristocrat who feared being alone on the long voyage. So, he brought along Charles Darwin as a companion. Together, they faced five years of physical and mental hardships. They battled the seas, explored dense Brazilian jungles and climbed inhospitable Andes mountains. By the end, Darwin had written a 770-page diary, with another 1,750 pages of notes. (He also had a collection of 5,436 skins, bones and carcasses.) These were published as the famous book *The Voyage of the Beagle*.

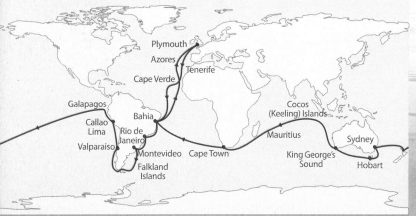

▶ *A painting of HMS Beagle in South America, by crewman Conrad Martens*

◀ *The Beagle set out from Plymouth, England, and made its way around South America to the Galapagos islands. From there, it crossed the Pacific, Indian and Atlantic oceans to reach England again*

The Galapagos Archipelago

Darwin spent about five weeks on the islands of Galapagos, admiring and recording their extraordinary wildlife. Many of the creatures here are endemic, which means that they cannot be found anywhere else on Earth.

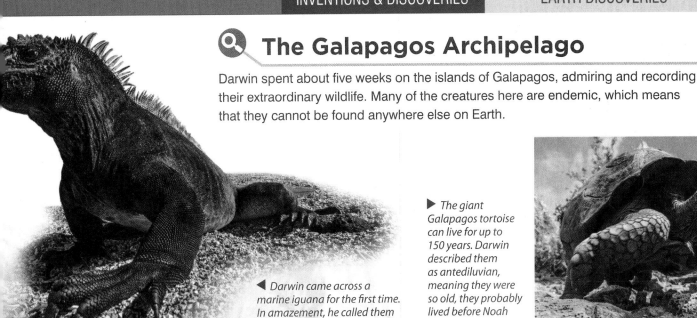

◀ *Darwin came across a marine iguana for the first time. In amazement, he called them 'imps of darkness'*

▶ *The giant Galapagos tortoise can live for up to 150 years. Darwin described them as antediluvian, meaning they were so old, they probably lived before Noah and the great flood*

Fossils

Darwin also discovered fossils of **extinct** animals in South America. Among them were the remains of giant sloths, mastodons, ancient armadillos and animals that looked like rhinoceroses and horses. Darwin concluded that animals that could not adapt to changing environments would die out. Until he propounded his theory, people believed that the fossils found in South America were of mythical creatures destroyed by the gods in an ancient time.

▶ *The giant sloth of South America was the size of an elephant*

▲ *A Galapagos sea lion*

Discovering Africa

David Livingstone (1813–1873) was a Scottish missionary whose explorations of the African heartland gave Europeans their first look into the continent. Livingstone's first trip lasted 15 years. He spent this time travelling tirelessly across Africa, meeting its people, spreading his teachings and condemning the abhorrent practice of slavery.

⊛ Incredible Individuals

During his 1844 trip, Livingstone courageously faced an attacking lion. His left arm was badly mauled. Eventually, he became unable to hold the barrel of his gun steadily. For the rest of his life, he was forced to fire from his left arm, and take aim using his left eye.

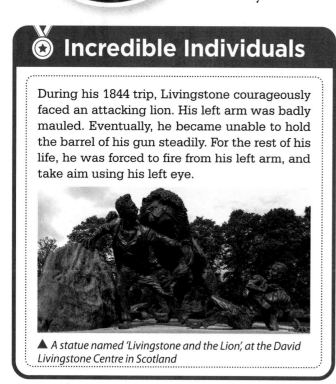

▲ *A statue named 'Livingstone and the Lion', at the David Livingstone Centre in Scotland*

▲ *A map of Dr Livingstone's westernmost explorations in Africa*

🔍 The Hero of Victoria Falls

Between November 1853 and May 1854, Livingstone made an arduous journey to discover a path from Linyanti to the Atlantic coast. He then returned to Linyanti again and struck out east, exploring the Zambezi regions. On 16 November, 1855, he came across a roaring, smoke-like waterfall on the Zambezi River. Claiming it for the British queen, he named it Victoria Falls. Livingstone returned to England and was received as a national hero.

▼ *On 1 August, 1849, Livingstone and a small company became the first Europeans to sight Lake Ngami*

▶ *Victoria Falls, a UNESCO World Heritage Site at Mosi-oa-Tunya National Park, Zambia*

In Real Life

The Zambezi mission furthered British colonial influence in Africa. In 1893, this area became the British Central Africa Protectorate. In 1907, it became Nyasaland. Finally, in 1966, it became the Republic of Malawi.

▲ Lake Malawi , surrounded by forested hills

Rivers Zambezi and Ruvuma

Livingstone returned to Africa in 1858 and stayed till 1864. This time, he came with a party of Europeans with whom he further explored the Zambezi. On 17 September, 1859, they became the first Britons to reach Ruvuma River. The mission helped amass a large and priceless body of scientific data.

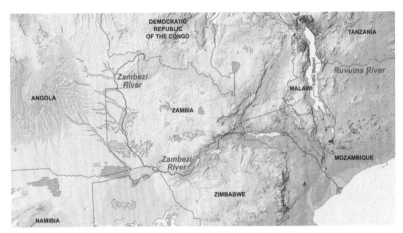

▲ The Zambezi River basin extends to Lake Malawi, which feeds the Ruvuma River

Farthest West

Livingstone was back in Africa by January 1866, exploring the area around Lake Tanganyika. At this time, his followers deserted him. They even cooked up stories about Livingstone's death. In the meantime, the man himself became the first European to reach Lake Mweru (1867) and Lake Bangweulu (1868). On 29 March, 1871, he reached Nyangwe on the Lualaba River, the greatest source of the Congo River. This was farther west than any European had travelled within Africa.

▲ Lake Bangweulu

At Rest in the South

Livingstone returned to Lake Tanganyika a sick man. Here, he was discovered by Henry M. Stanley, a reporter for the *New York Herald*. Stanley brought him much-needed medicine. Livingstone recovered, but refused to return home with Stanley. Instead, he journeyed south again. In May 1873, at Chitambo (northern Zambia), Africans found Livingstone dead by his bedside, kneeling as if in prayer. His body was taken back to England and buried with ceremony in Westminster Abbey.

In Real Life

Livingstone's geographical, technical and medical discoveries are still being studied today. In spite of the prejudices of the time, Livingstone worked fervently for the emancipation of slaves and believed in Africa's potential as a modern state.

▲ Stanley in Africa, around the time he met Livingstone

◀ The illustration depicts the meeting of Stanley and Livingstone

Undercover Adventures

An English spy named Sir Richard Francis Burton (1821–1890) was the first European to see Lake Tanganyika (in Africa) and a number of Islamic cities that were forbidden to Westerners. Over his lifetime, he wrote 43 travel books. He also translated 30 books from other languages. Most famous among them is an amazing 16-volume edition of *The Arabian Nights*.

▲ *The young scholar and spy Richard Burton*

▲ *Demons, angels, murderers and mythical beasts from Burton's translation of The Arabian Nights*

Mecca and Medina

In 1853, Burton dressed as a Pathan (an Afghan Muslim) and travelled to Cairo, Egypt. He made his way to Arabia to visit the sacred Medina. Following bandit-infested roads, Burton then travelled on to Mecca. At the time, no foreigners were allowed inside these two holiest of Islamic cities.

Facing a death sentence if he were caught, Burton snuck into the shrine of Ka'bah. He even sketched an accurate floor plan of this most sacred shrine of Islam. Burton published his journey as the *Pilgrimage to Al-Madinah and Mecca*. For the first time, people in the West saw the customs and manners of their Muslim contemporaries.

⊙ Incredible Individuals

Burton went to India in 1842 and became an intelligence officer—a spy! His job included visiting bazaars in disguise. There, he would secretly collect information from Muslim merchants. Over eight years, he mastered Arabic, Hindi, Marathi, Sindhi, Punjabi, Pashto, Telugu and Multani. By the end of his life he knew 25 languages and 40 dialects!

◄ *The shrine at Mecca packed with people*

► *Richard Burton disguised as a Muslim man*

African Adventures

In 1854, Burton became the first European to enter the forbidden East African city of Harar, without being executed. In 1857–1858, he went hunting for the source of the Nile River. The leader of the expedition was John Speke. Although they failed to find the source, Speke pushed on northeast and discovered the magnificent Lake Victoria.

▲ John Speke with Lake Victoria behind him

West Africa

In the 1860s, Burton was living in Fernando Po, an island near West Africa. During this time, he made frequent trips to the mainland and wrote five books about West African customs. These included fascinating discoveries about birth and death rituals, weddings, cannibalism and ritual murders. Burton's writings made him very popular with scholars, but the government thought he was mad.

Banishment and Books

Calling him dangerous, the government banished Burton far from his beloved Africa and India. Burton spent his time writing more books. In 1870, he published a translation titled *Vikram and the Vampire, or Tales of Hindu Devilry*. He also wrote a volume on the Sindh, two volumes on the gold mines of Midian and a number of other titles. Burton risked imprisonment by translating many lovely books that were considered immoral by the rulers of Britain. Finally, in 1886, the government recognised the value of his life's work. In February, he was knighted by Queen Victoria.

◄ *The fantastical artwork for Vikram and the Vampire, or Tales of Hindu Devilry were done by Ernest Griset*

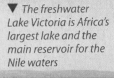

▼ *The freshwater Lake Victoria is Africa's largest lake and the main reservoir for the Nile waters*

► *Burton's tomb at Mortlake, London*

Around the World in 72 Days

Nellie Bly (1864–1922) was the most accomplished female journalist of her time. She lived a life full of adventure, and became famous by beating the fictional record for time taken to travel around the world.

The Fearless Journalist

Elizabeth Cochrane—better known as Nellie Bly—wrote articles that were phenomenal and profound. She first wrote on the condition of working girls and slum life. In 1886–1887, she spent months in Mexico, reporting on government corruption. Her sharply critical articles angered Mexican officials and caused her expulsion from the country. In 1887, she faked insanity to get into an asylum and report about how the mentally ill were being mistreated. Bly made similar forays into factories, prisons and even the legislature. Her work caught the attention of the public and brought about great social improvements. These important articles are now published as the books *Six Months in Mexico* and *Ten Days in a Madhouse*.

▼ *Bly's trip made her so famous, there was a popular board game 'Round the World With Nellie Bly' named after her*

Isn't It Amazing!

Bly's career began in 1885 when she sent an angry letter to the editor of the *Pittsburgh Dispatch*, against a mean-spirited article written about women. The editor was so impressed by her letter, he gave her a job as a reporter!

▶ *A 21-year-old Bly in Mexico*

Racing Jules

In 1873, Jules Verne published his travel-adventure novel, *Around the World in Eighty Days*. In the story, fictional hero Phileas Fogg wins a bet by accomplishing the titular journey. In 1889, Nellie Bly was invited to beat this fictional record. Nearly a million people entered a guessing contest on how long she would take to complete the race. On 14 November, Bly sailed out of New York. She boarded ships, trains, rickshaws, **sampans**, horses and **burros** all along her fantastic race. She finally returned to New York on a special train and was greeted by brass bands and fireworks. Her record was 72 days, 6 hours, 11 minutes and 14 seconds.

▼ *Bly's report on the Blackwell Island asylum's conditions caused a grand-jury investigation and led to improved standards in patient care*

▶ *Nellie Bly's reception at the end of her journey*

The Lost Cities of the Incas

Machu Picchu is an ancient place high in the Andes mountains of South America. It was once home to the Incas. The ruins of Machu Picchu were discovered by German adventurer Augusto Berns in 1867. But the world did not hear about it until American archaeologist Hiram Bingham (1875–1956) began his explorations.

▶ *The ruins of Machu Picchu, hidden in the Peruvian Andes, high above the Urubamba River valley*

🔍 The Search for Machu Picchu

In July 1911, Bingham led a hunt for Vilcabamba, the 'lost city of the Incas'. Vilcabamba was their name for a 16th-century mountain stronghold. Its location was a secret known only to the Incas. (They used it to fight against Spanish conquerors.) About 400 years later, the only clue to the city was a rumour, which said it was somewhere near Cuzco, in Peru.

At Cuzco, locals told Bingham to search the Urubamba River valley for the legendary Choquequirao (Cradle of Gold). Bingham had to trek 2,350 metres up into the formidable Andes. On July 24, the Quechua-speaking Melchor Arteaga led him to spectacular Incan ruins that lay in a saddle between the peaks Machu Picchu (Old Peak) and Huayna Picchu (New Peak).

▲ *Melchor Arteaga crossing the Urubamba River, 24 July, 1911*

🔍 An Incan Fortress City

In 1912 and 1915, Bingham led expert teams to Machu Picchu. They realised that the site was a vast palace complex belonging to the ruler Pachacuti Inca Yupanqui (ruled 1438–1471). The city was built using thousands of stone-cut steps, high walls, mysterious tunnels and other inventive structures!

▼ *Remains of Incan buildings at Machu Picchu*

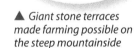

▼ *Dry stone walls of the Temple of the Sun, Machu Picchu*

▲ *Giant stone terraces made farming possible on the steep mountainside*

⭐ Incredible Individuals

Bingham's explorations also revealed the nearby sites of Vitcos and Espiritu Pampa. Gene Savoy, another American archaeologist, proved that Espiritu Pampa was in fact the real Vilcabamba. Over his lifetime, Savoy worked on more than 40 Incan and pre-Incan sites in Peru.

Cool Conquests

Roald Amundsen (1872–1928) was an explorer from Norway. He was the first person to reach the South Pole. He was also the first person to navigate a ship through the elusive Northwest Passage. Amundsen is one of the greatest figures in the history of polar exploration.

◀ The stake on the right marks the South Pole, while the board marks the achievements of explorers Roald Amundsen and Robert Scott

The Northwest Passage

The Passage was a shortcut from the Atlantic Ocean to the Pacific Ocean by sailing across the Arctic region. People believed that such a route lay above the coasts of modern Canada. Yet its exact location was a mystery.

Amundsen's Way

In 1903, Roald Amundsen took up the challenge. His goal was to sail through the Northwest Passage and around the northern Canadian coast. After a long, hard journey, Amundsen was able to reach Cape Colborne in August 1905. By the following month he had completed the greater part of the passage. At this point, he was stopped by winter and ice. The crew was forced to stay at Herschel Island in the Yukon. Once the ice melted, they resumed their journey. Late in August 1906, they completed the route at Nome, Alaska. Amundsen was given a hero's welcome for his successful discovery of the passage!

Isn't It Amazing!

Explorers had been searching for the Northwest Passage for centuries! As far back as 1497, King Henry VII of England sent John Cabot in search of a northwest passage to eastern Asia. His explorations led to British claims over Canada.

▲ A depiction of John Cabot departing Bristol to explore the Americas

◀ To conquer the Northwest Passage, Amundsen sailed out with six men on a 42,637-kilogram sloop named Gjöa

▲ Christmas dinner for the Gjöa crew, 1903

◀ Amundsen and his crew aboard the Gjöa at the end of the trip at Nome (Alaska) on 1 September, 1906

🔍 South Pole

In June 1910, Amundsen headed for the South Pole. Sailing the Fram Strait, he reached the Bay of Whale in Antarctica and set up a base camp. Experienced in the ways of ice and snow, Amundsen carefully prepared for the journey. He knew that accidents were common on polar lands. So, he made a trip halfway to the pole, to store emergency food supplies all along the way. He used sled dogs to transport his supplies.

▲ The crew sewing polar kits in the living room of the Fram

▲ One of the food deposits; Amundsen laid down about 2,721 kg of supplies, equipment and fuel

▲ On the way to the South Pole

🔍 The Historic Trip

On 19 October, 1911, Amundsen set out with four men, four sledges and 52 dogs. The weather was on their side for the next couple of months. The group reached the South Pole on 14 December. The explorers stayed there until the 17th, making scientific observations. They safely returned to the Bay of Whales on 25 January, 1912.

▲ Roald Amundsen, Helmer Hanssen, Sverre Hassel and Oscar Wisting at the South Pole on 17 December, 1911

▼ Robert Scott's team at the South Pole

⊛ Incredible Individuals

A rival team of explorers was chasing the South Pole at the same time as Amundsen. It was led by the English explorer Robert Scott. This group's base camp was 100 kilometres farther from the pole than Amundsen's. Also, they used ponies instead of sled dogs for transport. Scott's team arrived at the South Pole on 17 January, 1913—one month after Amundsen. Tragically, Scott's team faced bad weather, ran out of food and fuel, and died in Antarctica.

The Race to the North Pole

The geographical North Pole is found at a latitude of 90° N. This is a point at which all the globe's longitudes come together. The ocean around it is covered with ice. The first person to try to reach the North Pole was Henry Hudson in 1607.

🔍 Early Polar Records

Almost 160 years later, the second attempt was made by a Russian named Vasily Yakovlevich Chichagov. He reached just north of 80° latitude. Barriers of ice forced him to turn back! Over 1771–1871, many explorers made a push for the pole, but none succeeded. In 1871, American Charles Francis Hall got as close as 82° N. Tragically, Hall passed away that winter, soon after his ship *Polaris* got stranded in ice.

◀ *The funeral of Captain Charles Francis Hall*

🔍 The Fram Revelation

In 1893, a crew led by Norwegian explorer Fridtjof Nansen sailed towards the pole. They were on the *Fram*, a ship specially designed to avoid getting crushed by ice. Nansen's idea was to intentionally sail into an ice pack! When this happened, the design of the ship raised it above the ice. The ship then drifted polewards for almost three years. A great deal of scientific information was collected at this time. Most importantly, people realised that the way to the North Pole was not via open sea; rather it was covered in ice. One could not simply get there by ship.

◀ *The Fram braving the Arctic ice*

🔍 The Fram Expedition's Record

Just by drifting, the *Fram* reached 84° N in 1896. At this point, Nansen and his crewman Hjalmar Johansen set off over the solid ice of Franz Josef Land on a sledge. They reached just beyond 86° N before winter set in and worsening conditions forced them to return.

▲ *The snow-covered hut in which Nansen and Johansen spent the winter of 1895–1896*

▼ *View from the solid ice at the pole, from the North Pole Web Cam, a part of the North Pole Environmental Observatory*

▲ *Nansen and Johansen preparing to depart the Fram for their sledge journey to the North Pole*

🔍 Controversial Claims

With the information from the *Fram*, a great race began. Explorers vied to be the first to reach the North Pole. In 1909, American Robert Peary claimed he had reached the pole from Cape Columbia. Just before Peary's return, another American named Fredrick A. Cook announced that he had reached the pole from Axel Heiberg Island, with the help of Inuits. However, neither of them could show proof of their claims. Both men's achievements are surrounded by doubt, even today.

▶ *Peary's team at what they claimed was the North Pole*

▲ *USS Skate surfacing in the Arctic, 1959*

🔍 Confirmed Records

On 12 May, 1926, Roald Amundsen set off from Spitsbergen in an airship and flew across the pole to Alaska. Along with him were Lincoln Ellsworth and Umberto Nobile. These are the first known people to have reached and crossed the North Pole. In 1958, the US nuclear submarine *Nautilus* reached the pole under water. The next year, nuclear submarine *Skate* reached the pole and surfaced. In 1968, an American team led by Ralph Plaisted visited the pole by snowmobile. In 1977, the powerful Soviet icebreaker ship *Arktika* sailed all the way to the pole from the New Siberian Islands.

▶ *Norge, the semi-rigid airship that flew Amundsen and team over the North Pole*

▼ *Russian Ivan Papanin, leader of the first expedition to set up an ice station at the North Pole, 1937*

◀ *The Russian nuclear icebreaker Arktika*

On Top of the World

▲ *In Nepal, Everest is called Sagarmatha. It lies in the UNESCO World Heritage Site of Sagarmatha National Park, a 1,234-square kilometre area that was set up in 1976*

The world's highest mountain above sea level is Mount Everest. It is 8,850 metres high and located in the Himalayas on the borders of Nepal and Tibet. The first people to reach its summit were New Zealand mountain climber Edmund Hillary (1919–2008) and Tibetan mountaineer Tenzing Norgay (1914–1986).

◀ *Vibrant fauna from around Sagarmatha, such as the blood pheasant (left) and the Himalayan monal (right)*

🔍 The First Expeditions

No human beings live on Everest. However, its valleys are home to Tibetan communities, like the Sherpas. They used to avoid climbing the high peaks, believing that gods and demons lived there. The first group to explore the area around Everest was a British team in 1921. In 1924, another team climbed as high as 8,546 metres. Until WWII began in 1939, many teams came to conquer Everest, but failed. However, they explored and mapped routes that made it possible for future teams to succeed.

👤 In Real Life

Since Hillary and Norgay's 1953 climb, more than 7,600 people have reached the peak of Everest. Tragically, some 300 mountaineers have died in the attempt.

◀ *Tenzing Norgay first attempted scaling Everest as part of a 1935 team when he was only 19 years old. Over the next few years, he took part in more Everest expeditions than anyone else*

▲ *In 1950, China took over Tibet and closed the northern route to Everest. In 1951, Nepal gave people permission to climb the mountain from its land*

💡 Isn't It Amazing!

If you measure a mountain from its foot to its peak, the tallest mountain in the world is Mauna Kea in Hawaii. It is 10,205 metres high. The part that you see is only 4,205 metres high. The rest of it lies under water!

▶ *The volcanic Mauna Kea, Hawaii*

🔍 The Steps to the Summit

On the Northeast Ridge of Everest, there are three formidable 'steps' just before the summit. These steps are steep rock faces that make it difficult to reach the peak. The First Step is a straight limestone wall about 34 metres high. Above it is a ledge. The Second Step begins here and is 50 metres high. In 1975, the Chinese actually fixed a ladder over it, to make the climb easier! The Third Step is sheer rock-face about 30 metres high. It leads to a slope that rises to the summit.

▶ A mountaineer skiing down the steep Northeast

🔍 The Ascent of 1953

A British team led by Colonel John Hunt and Baron Hunt set out for Everest in 1953. On 28 May, they set up a camp for the night at 8,500 metres. Hillary and Norgay set out for the summit early next morning. After hours of brutal trekking, they reached the peak of Everest at 11:30 am. The men shook hands and hugged each other. Hillary took photos and left a crucifix. Tenzing, a Buddhist, made offerings to the mountain. The two men ate some sweets and spent about 15 minutes on top of the world. By 2 June, the entire team was back at the base camp. The joyous news broke out in London on the same day that Queen Elizabeth II was crowned! Edmund Hillary wrote about his journey in High Adventure (1955). He came back to the Everest region many times in the early 1960s, but never again climbed the peak. Time Magazine named him and Tenzing Norgay among the 100 most influential people of the 20th century.

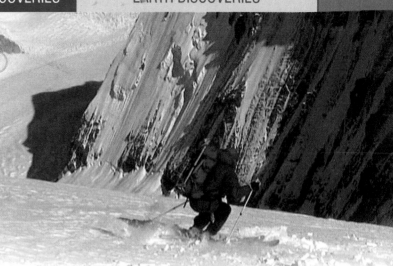

▲ The first photos of Everest were taken from airplanes in 1933

▶ The north face of the Everest showing the location of the Three Steps

1st 2nd 3rd

◀ The two photographs show Tenzing Norgay and Edmund Hillary during and after their historical climb

Word Check

Admiral: The chief commander of a navy

Bay: It is a small body of water surrounded by land on three sides.

Blubber: It is the fat of mammals of the sea, such as whales and seals.

Burro: It is a small donkey.

Cartography: It is the art and science of map-making.

Conquistador: It is a title used to describe a leader in the Spanish conquest of the Americas.

Corps: It is a military unit.

Envoy or ambassador: A person who represents his or her government in a foreign nation

Estuary: It refers to the widening arms of a river, where they meet the sea.

Expedition: It is a journey with a specific goal, usually undertaken with a group of people.

Extinct: It means that an animal or plant is no longer in existence.

Gulf: It is a part of the sea that is surrounded by land on three sides. It is larger than a bay.

Indigenous: It refers to a group of people who are native to an area.

Isthmus: It is a narrow strip of land surrounded by water on two sides.

Kinsay: It is a city that was captured by the Mongols in 1279. It helped them control all of China. With more than a million people, it was the world's largest city at the time—many times larger than the cities of Europe.

Lacquerware: These are decorative wooden objects painted with a glossy varnish called lacquer.

Marooned: It means to abandon a person on a deserted island.

Mutiny: It is a revolt against a superior officer.

Pilgrimage: It is a journey to a sacred place.

Sampans: They are narrow wooden boats used in East Asia.

Strait: It is a narrow strip of water surrounded by land on two sides.